Jack

gains two pounds every month.

Ashley

is the most sentimental of all.

Paul

dreams only of setting sail.

Jason

loves artistic activities.

LEARN-A-WORD BOOKS
IN ENGLISH, FRENCH & SPANISH

In the Country

383 Words in English, French & Spanish

Text by Alain Grée
Illustrations by Luis Camps

DERRYDALE BOOKS • NEW YORK

Art copyright © 1973 by Casterman. English Translation copyright © 1986 by OBC, Inc. Originally published in French under the title *Les Farfeluches à la Campagne*. All rights reserved. This 1986 edition is published by Derrydale Books, distributed by Crown Publishers, Inc., by arrangement with Casterman. Printed and Bound in Belgium.
Library of Congress Cataloging-in-Publication Data
Grée, Alain. In the country. (Learn-a-word books in English, French & Spanish). Translation of: Les farfeluches à la campagne. English, French, and Spanish.
 Summary: A group of kids known as "The Rascals" enjoy the many activities on the farm. Includes brief running text and detailed illustrations with each item labeled in English, French, and Spanish. Also features games and related activities.
 1. Farm life—Juvenile literature. 2. Picture dictionaries, Polyglot—Juvenile literature. [1. Farm life. 2. Picture dictionaries, Polyglot] I. Camps, Luis. II. Title. III. Series: Grée, Alain. Learn-a-word books in English, French & Spanish.
S519.G6512 1986 630 86-8921 ISBN 0-517-61498-7 h g f e d c b a

A Country Landscape

After a night sleeping under the stars, Justine's breakfast is a welcome treat for the Rascals. Afterward they will visit the mill, chat with the fisherman, photograph the viaduct, explore the castle, and, finally, visit Uncle Bill on his farm.

mountain
montagne
montaña

village
village
pueblo

hill
colline
colina

train
train
tren

tunnel
tunnel
túnel

viaduct
viaduc
viaducto

station
gare
estación

scarecrow
épouvantail
espantapájaros

mill
moulin à eau
molino

river
rivière
río

bridge
pont
puente

rowboat
barque
barca

crossroads
carrefour
cruce

road sign
panneau routier
señal de carretera

truck
camion
camión

car
voiture
coche

road
route
ruta

fruit trees
arbres fruitiers
árboles frutales

hedge
haie
seto

meadow
pré
prado

sheep
moutons
ovejas

gun
fusil
escopeta

hunter
chasseur
cazador

dog
chien
perro

plowed field
champ labouré
campo arado

ladder
échelle
escalera

4

clouds
nuages
nubes

airplane
avion
avión

castle
château
castillo

path
chemin
senda

forest
bosquet
bosque

farm
ferme
finca

tree
arbre
árbol

cow
vache
vaca

haystack
meule
pajar

tractor
tracteur
tractor

hay
paille
paja

pine tree
sapin
pino

bird
oiseau
pájaro

horse
cheval
caballo

backpack
sac à dos
mochila

camp stove
réchaud
estufa

sausages
saucisses
salchichas

tent
tente de camping
tienda de campaña

5

windmill
roue éolienne
molino de viento

pigeons
pigeons
palomas

chimney
cheminée
chimenea

lightning rod
paratonnerre
pararrayos

hayloft
grenier
granero

tile roof
toit de tuiles
tejado de tejas

cow
vache
vaca

pulley
poulie
polea

sacks
sacs
sacos

ladder
échelle
escalera

birdhouse
nichoir
nidal

ring
anneau
anillo

portico
hangar
pórtico

beams
poutres
vigas

bolt
verrou
cerradura

cowshed
étable
establo de vacas

ax
hache
hacha

stable
écurie
establo

bales of hay
bottes de foin
botes de heno

block
billot
tronco

milk can
bidon de lait
bidón de leche

chicks
poussins
polluelos

woodpile
tas de bois
montón de leña

goat
chèvre
cabra

bucket
seau
balde

hen
poule
gallina

water trough
abreuvoir
abrevadero

wheel
roue
rueda

6

weathervane
girouette
veleta

apple tree
pommier
manzano

thatched roof
toit de chaume
techado de paja

dormer window
lucarne
buharda

lamp
lanterne
farol

shutter
volet
contra ventana

stairs
escalier
escalera

pigs
porcs
cochinos

Dutch door
porte coupée
puerta cortada

window
fenêtre
ventana

flowers
fleurs
flores

pig sty
porcherie
pocilga

barrel
tonneau
barril

flower box
bac a fleurs
caja de flores

pitchfork
fourche
horca

flag
drapeau
bandera

rope
corde
soga

cart
charrette
carro

The Barnyard

Uncle Bill has lots of work to do, so he is happy to accept the Rascals' offer to help. To start, the animals have to be fed. No sooner said than done! But why raise the cow up to the hayloft? Wouldn't it be easier to bring the hay down to the stalls? The Rascals sure have some funny ideas!

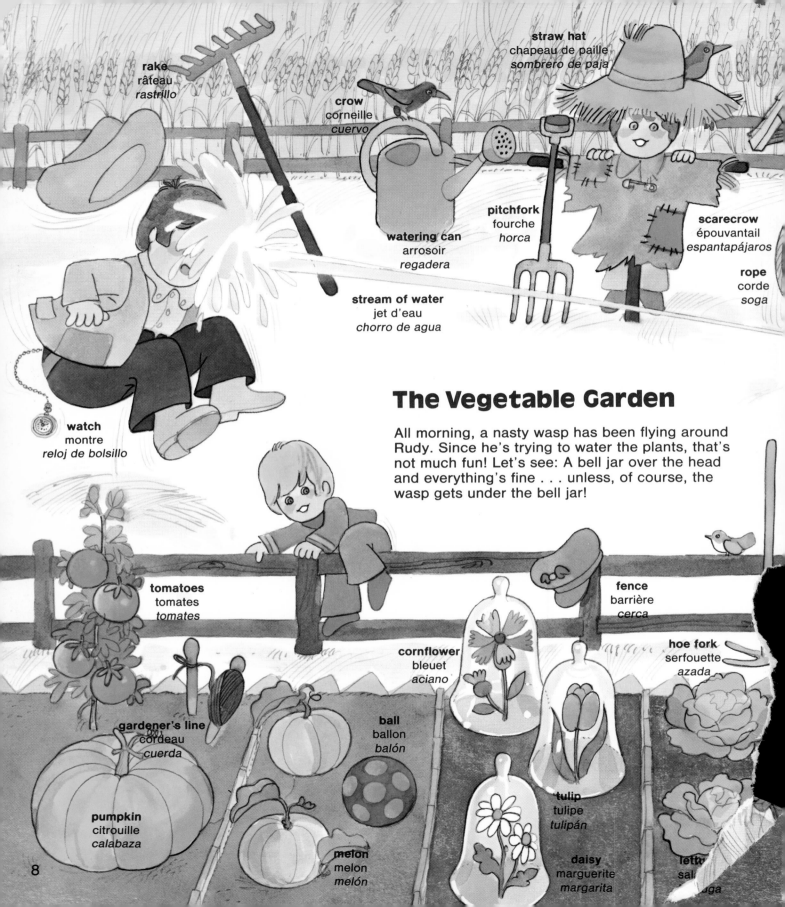

rake
râteau
rastrillo

crow
corneille
cuervo

straw hat
chapeau de paille
sombrero de paja

watering can
arrosoir
regadera

pitchfork
fourche
horca

scarecrow
épouvantail
espantapájaros

rope
corde
soga

stream of water
jet d'eau
chorro de agua

watch
montre
reloj de bolsillo

The Vegetable Garden

All morning, a nasty wasp has been flying around Rudy. Since he's trying to water the plants, that's not much fun! Let's see: A bell jar over the head and everything's fine . . . unless, of course, the wasp gets under the bell jar!

tomatoes
tomates
tomates

fence
barrière
cerca

cornflower
bleuet
aciano

hoe fork
serfouette
azada

gardener's line
cordeau
cuerda

ball
ballon
balón

pumpkin
citrouille
calabaza

tulip
tulipe
tulipán

melon
melon
melón

daisy
marguerite
margarita

lettu
sal
uga

8

wheat field
champ de blé
campo de trigo

swing
balançoire
columpio

bucket
seau
cubo

bell jar
cloche
campana

faucet
robinet
grifo

ear of wheat
épi
espiga

well
puits
pozo

bag of fertilizer
sac d'engrais
saco de abono

hoe
binette
azada

watering hose
tuyau d'arrosage
mangera

hook
crochet
gancho

peppers
poivrons
pimientos

leek
poireaux
puerro

knife
couteau
cuchillo

frying pan
poêle
sartén

path
allée
vereda

crate
caisse
caja

sack
sac
saco

carrots
carottes
zanahorias

planting tool
plantor
plantador

pruning shears
sécateur
podaderas

plank
planche
tabla

9

chicken wire
grillage
alambrado

wheelbarrow
brouette
carretilla

butterfly
papillon
mariposa

bird
oiseau
pájaro

trowel
truelle
trulla

bush
arbuste
arbusto

cement
ciment
cemento

pick
pioche
pico

ax
hache
hacha

ladder
échelle
escalera

hat
chapeau
sombrero

posts
pieux
palos

door
porte
puerta

lock
serrure
cerradura

donkey
ane
asno

sledgehammer
masse
maso

mushrooms
champignons
setas

pincers
tenailles
tenazas

10

cap
bonnet
gorro

pipe
pipe
pipa

logs
bûches
leña

leaf
feuille
hoja

hand saw
scie égoïne
serrucho

trunk
tronc
tronco

sawdust
sciure
serrín

stump
souche
tronco

bundle
fagot
haz

chain saw
tronçonneuse
sierra de cadena

ladle
louche
cucharón

plates
assiettes
platos

pencil
crayon
lápiz

nails
clous
clavos

pot
fait-tout
olla

sausage
saucisson
salchichón

bread
pain
pan

wood fire
feu de bois
fuego de leña

glasses
gobelets
vasos

Putting Up a Fence

It's time to stop fooling around. The Rascals help Uncle
Bill build a fence around the pasture. Some posts, some
chicken wire, some nails. . . . Oops! It looks like
Justine's soup will have plenty of iron in it!

camp stool
pliant
taburete doblegable

knife
couteau
cuchillo

11

autumn foliage
feuillage d'automne
follaje de otoño

sword
épée
espada

mouse
souris
ratón

pigeon house
pigeonnier
palomar

pigeon
pigeon
paloma

chicken coop
poulailler
gallinera

eggs
oeufs
huevos

hen
poule
gallina

perch
perchoir
percha

guinea hen
pintade
gallina de guinea

fence
clôture
vallado

rooster
coq
gallo

drake
canard
pato

ducklings
canetons
patitos

The Little Farm Animals

On a farm, all of the animals have a special place to live. The bees live in a hive, the rabbits in a hutch. The chickens live in a coop, the pigeons in a pigeon house, and the ducks in a pond. How do we recognize a duck? By its webbed feet, of course!

12

bees
abeilles
abejas

shed
remise
depósito

beehive
ruche
colmena

orn crib
e à maïs
a de maíz

rabbit hutch
clapier
conejera

smoker
enfumoir
ahumador

chicks
poussins
polluelas

grain sack
sac de grain
saco de granos

handlebars
guidon
manillar

grain
grain
granos

pump
pompe
bomba de agua

wagon
chariot
carro

bicycle
bicyclette
bicicleta

fishing rod
canne à pêche
caña de pescar

bucket
seau
cabo

birdhouse
nichoir
nidal

fence
barrière
cerca

face mask
masque
máscara

flipper
palme
aleta

reel
moulinet
carreta de pescar

goose
oie
gansa

tortoise
tortue
tortuga

snail
escargot
caracol

bench
banc
banco

rhododendron
rhododendron
rododendro

13

crow
corneille
cuervo

pheasant
faisan
faisán

pole
perche
palo

butterfly net
filet à papillons
red de mariposas

fruits
fruits
frutas

green plums
prunes verts
ciruelas verdes

crate
caisse
caja

barrel
tonneau
barril

tree
arbre
árbol

dragonfly
libellule
libélula

peaches
pêches
melocotones

quinces
coings
membrillos

pears
poires
peras

apples
pommes
manzana

crate
cageot
caja

wheelbarrow
brouette
carretilla

basket
panier
cesta

strawberries
fraises
frutillas

currants
groseilles
grosellas

raspberries
framboises
frambuesas

worm
ver
gusano

hazelnuts
noisettes
avellanas

tennis ball
balle de tennis
pelota de tenis

14

feathered hat
chapeau à plumes
sombrero a plumas

rapier
rapière
estoque

target
cible
blanco

arrow
flèche
flecha

wasp
guêpe
avispa

bow
arc
arco

cap
casquette
gorro

stool
tabouret
taburete

step ladder
escabeau
escalera

walnuts
noix
nueces

sack
sac
saco

figs
figues
higos

apricots
abricots
albaricoques

racket
raquette
raqueta

Picking Fruit in the Orchard

Mr. Morris, who was playing tennis next door, has
quite a problem: His ball landed in the orchard.
But with all the fruit around, how can he find it?

cherries
cerises
cerezas

15

The Crops

Vegetables, fruits, grains . . . perfect models for a painter! Jason is delighted. As for Uncle Bill's dog, he has discovered a great truth: A picture is worth a thousand words!

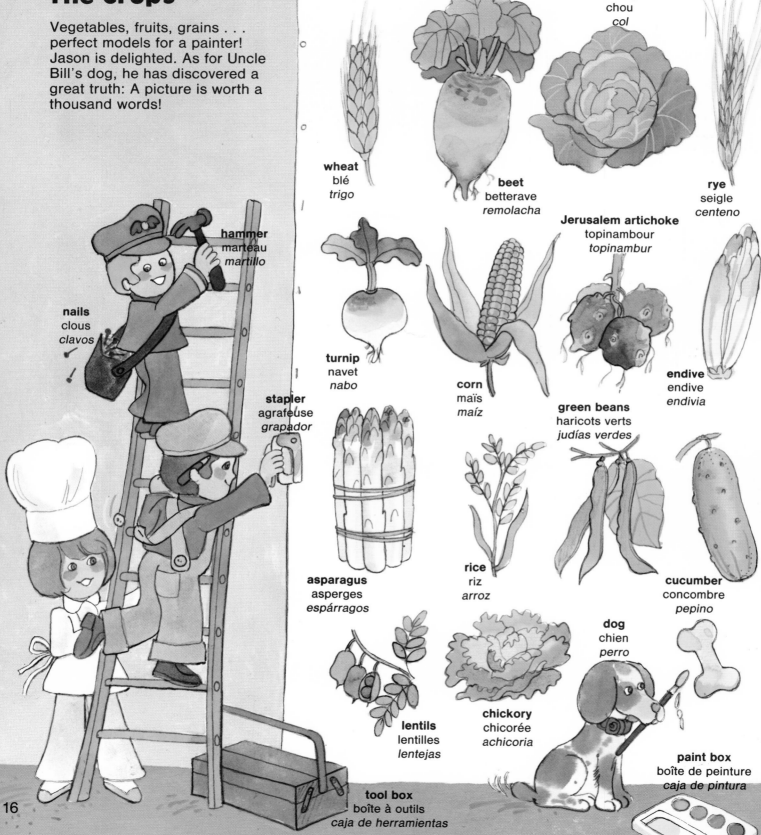

wheat
blé
trigo

cabbage
chou
col

beet
betterave
remolacha

rye
seigle
centeno

Jerusalem artichoke
topinambour
topinambur

turnip
navet
nabo

corn
maïs
maíz

endive
endive
endivia

green beans
haricots verts
judías verdes

asparagus
asperges
espárragos

rice
riz
arroz

cucumber
concombre
pepino

hammer
marteau
martillo

nails
clous
clavos

stapler
agrafeuse
grapador

lentils
lentilles
lentejas

chickory
chicorée
achicoria

dog
chien
perro

paint box
boîte de peinture
caja de pintura

tool box
boîte à outils
caja de herramientas

16

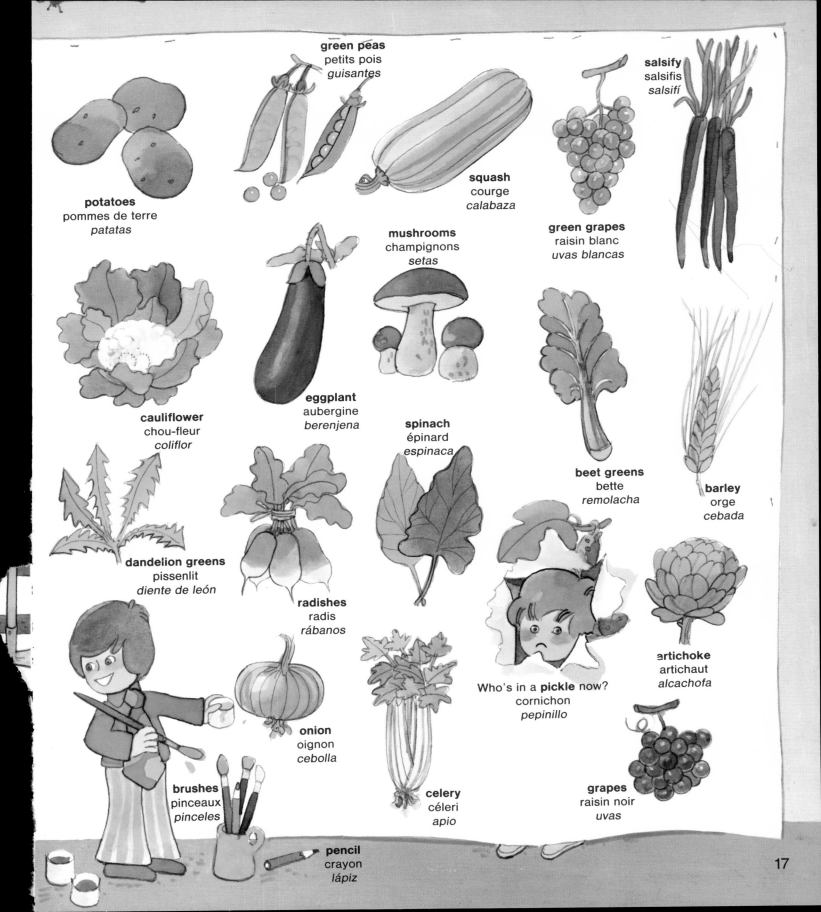

green peas
petits pois
guisantes

salsify
salsifis
salsifí

potatoes
pommes de terre
patatas

squash
courge
calabaza

mushrooms
champignons
setas

green grapes
raisin blanc
uvas blancas

cauliflower
chou-fleur
coliflor

eggplant
aubergine
berenjena

spinach
épinard
espinaca

beet greens
bette
remolacha

barley
orge
cebada

dandelion greens
pissenlit
diente de león

radishes
radis
rábanos

artichoke
artichaut
alcachofa

Who's in a **pickle** now?
cornichon
pepinillo

onion
oignon
cebolla

brushes
pinceaux
pinceles

celery
céleri
apio

grapes
raisin noir
uvas

pencil
crayon
lápiz

17

beam
poutre
viga

brush
pinceau
pincel

lamp
lampe
farol

chain
chaîne
cadena

barrel
tonneau
barril

door
porte
puerta

hinge
gond
bisagra

shears
cisaille
podaderas

paint can
pot de peinture
bote de pintura

rope
corde
soga

broom
balai
escoba

chicken
poulet
pollo

ax
hache
hacha

spigot
cannelle
canilla

vat
cuve
cava

block
billot
tronco

bottle
bouteille
botella

shovel
pelle
pala

lawnmower
tondeuse à gazon
máquina corta cesped

The Tool Shed

The mice are still in a state of shock! There they were, living happily in the tool shed, until the Rascals came along and turned everything upside down. Even the donkey is very upset. And what will Uncle Bill say?

string
ficelle
cuerda

billhook
serpe
machete

18

birdcage
cage à oiseau
jaula

dart
flechette
dado

jug
cruchon
cántaro

paint cans
pots de peinture
bote de pintura

roller
rouleau
rodillo

caliper
compas
compás

shelf
étagère
estante

square
équerre
cantonera

saw
scie
serrucho

window pane
vitre
vidrio

bird
oiseau
pájaro

donkey
âne
asno

boards
planches
tablas

chisel
ciseau à bois
escoplo

file
lime
lima

fly
mouche
mosca

hammer
marteau
martillo

pincers
tenailles
tenazas

mallet
maillet
mallo

workbench
établi
banco de trabajo

screwdriver
tournevis
destornillador

plane
rabot
cepillo

drawers
tiroirs
gavetas

vise
presse
prensa de banco

oil can
bidon d'huile
lata de aceite

wire
fil de fer
cable de hierro

brace
vilebrequin
berbiquí

wheel
roue
rueda

stool
tabouret
taburete

sickle
faucille
hoz

19

spotlight
projecteur
luz concentrada

movie camera
caméra
cámara

binoculars
jumelles
prismáticos

number
dossard
número de espalda

electric cord
fil electrique
cable eléctrico

film maker
cinéaste
cineasta

riding crop
cravache
látigo

horn
corne
cuerno

rein
rêne
riendas

cow
vache
vaca

bit
mors
brida

horse
cheval
caballo

cow bell
clochette
cencerro

dog
chien
perro

calf
veau
ternera

farmer
fermier
agricultor

pitchfork
fourche
horca

A Lively Departure

To celebrate their departure, the Rascals have organized a race with the farm animals. The contestants are on the starting line . . . ready . . . set . . . . Hey, there's the farmer crossing the race track! Stop, stop! Too late, they're on their way!

20

shield
bouclier
escudo

helmet
heaume
yelmo

banner
banderole
bandera

armor
armure
armadura

brush
pinceau
pincel

ram
bélier
carnero

goat
chèvre
cabra

smoke
fumée
humo

dust
poussière
polvo

revolver
revolver
revólver

helmet
casque
casco

parachute
parachute
paracaidas

lance
lance
lanza

starting line
ligne de départ
punto de partida

stirrup
étrier
estribo

saddle
selle
silla de montar

pencil
crayon
lápiz

horseshoes
fers
hierros

flag
drapeau
bandera

shoe
soulier
zapato

donkey
âne
asno

pig
cochon
cochino

trophy
coupe
trofeo

carrot
carotte
zanahoria

21

Justine

is already a perfect homemaker.

Patrick

fights imaginary bandits.

Rudy

is only happy with a hammer
in his hand.

Junior

is seventy-five pounds of muscle.

Max

hopes to be a pilot someday.

Peter

is more absent-minded
than clumsy.